SEVEN OSMOTIC
B E I N G S

we are not what we see, this world ain't what is taught

Ashwini Kumar Aggarwal

जय गुँरुदेव

ISBN13: 978-93-92201-42-4 Paperback Edition
ISBN13: 978-93-92201-43-1 Hardbound Edition
ISBN13: 978-93-92201-48-6 Digital Edition

Title: **Seven Osmotic Beings**
Author: **Ashwini Kumar Aggarwal**

Printed and Published by
Devotees of Sri Sri Ravi Shankar Ashram
34 Sunny Enclave, Devigarh Road,
Patiala 147001, Punjab, India

https://advaita56.weebly.com/
The Art of Living Centre

https://www.artofliving.org/

5th August 2021, Fabulous Meeting with Lord at Sri Sri School of Yoga front lawn alongwith SSRVM Trustees, Dvadashi Tithi, Pradosh Vrat, Krishna Paksha, Shravan Masa, Varsha Ritu, Ardra Nakshatra. Vikram Samvat 2078 Ananda, Saka Era 1943 Plava
(On 5th Aug 1969, Mariner 7 spacecraft flies 3430 Km above Mars)

1st Edition August 2021

जय गुरुदेव

Dedication

Sri Sri Ravi Shankar

dreamers make it BIG

Acknowledgements

Fabulous meeting with Lord at Sri Sri School of Yoga front lawn alongwith SSRVM Trustees on 5th August at 11am. Lord came from the far side and sat on the chair facing block of https://srisrischoolofyoga.org/. I was alone, on the edge, at the road going to Sambasada Shiva temple. He waved to me with a beaming smile, drenching me with joy and nectarine grace. Preeti and Banka had taken me to Bangalore Ashram and we stayed in Baliga quarters adjacent to Times of India Tripura building from 4-7th August.

Front Cover Photo Credits

Photo by Ivan Samkov from Pexels:
https://www.pexels.com/photo/woman-in-black-tank-top-raising-her-hands-5254986/

Blessing

All that you can do is to raise the level of Sattva. And then when Sattva's level is high, we have to wait one moment, any moment knowledge can dawn there.

All that you can do to have sunlight in this room, is to open the curtains and keep the windows open. And when dawn comes, it just dawns. You have the sunlight inside.

Sri Sri Ravi Shankar
A discourse on Yogasara Upanishad

Prayer

O Unknown dear!
May i touch THE eternityβ
May i travel seamlesslyα
May i support and belong to whomsoever it isδ

Someday TIME SPACE CONSCIOUSNESS trio is exited→
yademoS SSENSUOICSNOC ECAPS EMIT

Contents

Osmosis

A Passive transport without energy expense.

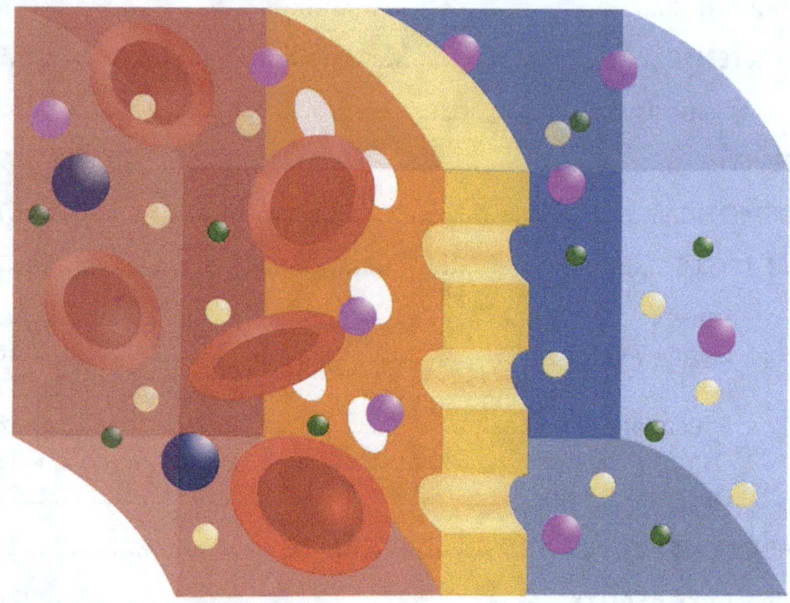

Freemesm, CC BY-SA 3.0 <https://creativecommons.org/licenses/by-sa/3.0>, via Wikimedia Commons

Unhindered passage of particles through a membrane net, based on size or speed, and also on **intent** and will**ing**ness.

Seven

Any number is valid, math is not finicky, numerical support as a basis for conversation, discussion, logic, nay emotion.

In principle,
- 7 chakras of aural body
- 7 layers of discrete consciousness
- 7 geographical continents on earth
- 7 senses in totality with memory and intuition
- 7 planets in jyotisha
- 7 genetic races
- 7 milestones of age

Osmotic

The Minimum energy needed to halt Osmosis.

Beings

Particles in the cosmos having an independent identity due to Osmotic pressure on Osmosis.

In principle, beings are distinct due to
- boundary based on size, e.g. mud pots
- color or dress or texture code, e.g. light spectrum
- form or shape or appearance, e.g. females, tigers
- name, even when identical otherwise, e.g. Lord, God
- shell, even when identical otherwise, e.g. electrons
- vibes they emit, e.g. emotion

Pots may be big or small, fat or shapely. Do they bother? Umm. Hard to say.

Being pattern based on **Vibes**

9

Bulbs may be colored variously. Do they bother? Yes definitely. Some colors are disliked by some, some colors fascinate others.

Offices, Shopping, Skyline can get heavy, monotonous, or delightful. Think about it.

With fog or limited visibility, the appearance changes dramatically.

Also, with snow cover.

Surely at dusk when the lights come on.

Ganesha Durga…both are God Lord Omnipotent. However, both evoke distinct emotions and are addressed differently.

Senses

We are supposed to have 5 senses, however in practice, all of us add memory and instinct, so what the brain receives is input from 7 sources.

1. Hearing
2. Touching
3. Seeing
4. Tasting
5. Smelling

6. Retrieving from m**em**o**ry**
7. Superimposing the **instin**ct

In principle, the input sources may get recalibrated
- in case of failure of any sense
- if memory has no information as in a new event
- or instinct is non-functional

In summary, we are based on these 7 inputs, their interplay and current impact, hence we are called Seven Osmotic Beings.

Eight = 7+1

8 aspects to learning or disseminating.
    8.   Hearing
    9.   Touching
    10. Seeing
    11. Tasting
    12. Smelling
    13. Retrieving from m**e**m**ory**
    14. Superimposing the **instin**ct (in**tui**tion)

    +1. Having an in**ten**t or willingness, also known as **grace**

Devi

The Devi stands complete with 8 arms and hands, or instructs with the 8 golden principles. Seers of yore taught in gurukuls and depicted the Mother Divine endowed with 8.

1. Blessing 2. Trident 3. Sword 4. SudarshanChakra 5. Conch 6. Mace 7. Bow-n-Arrow 8. Lotus.

Education

Most education is based on physical parameters alone, i.e. just the 5 senses, minus memory and intuition. Hence it lacks entirely in arriving at the fundamental truth, nay, education presents an incorrect or invalid aspect of life, our planet, and time and space and consciousness.

Education needs to be reinvented and revamped, keeping in mind the composite nature of this creation. Education cannot achieve any aim, if the classrooms and class teachers lack the basics.

Education must be infused with the 8 golden principles. Children must be taught by exposing to and reinforcing the 8 aspects.
1. Hearing correctly
2. Touching properly
3. Seeing clearly
4. Tasting deliciously
5. Smelling deeply
6. Retrieving facts from memory
7. Superimposing one's native instinct

+1. Probing and being honest with one's intent, intuition, or willingness to learn *or not to learn*. This is simply discarded as the term "she got lucky", rather it must be addressed by the school platform and environment in a wholesome manner.

Osmosis Happens

Whichever sense+memory+instinct of the 7 is more concentrated, tends to permeate into the other by Osmosis.

If **H^1**earing is solely being relied upon, *as in a phone call*, it shall color the other senses and memory as well.

If **S^2**ight is very important in the present while watching a thrilling cricket match, it shall overflow and flood the rest 7 too.

Similarly **T^3**ouch in romance or during love-making overpowers the remaining inputs and instincts.

A^{4}roma during supper is a precondition for taste as well as appetite, smell is the Lord at this juncture.

Without **T^5**aste, even the best foods shall not get digested nor assimilated by the body.

On the other hand, if a deep **M^6**emory gets triggered, the rest take a backseat.

And if the **I^7**nstinct comes into play, then nothing else works.

Opposite Values

We have heard, applied or marveled at the law of creation: OPPOSITE VALUES ARE COMPLEMENTARY IN NATURE.

Have you also noticed that Space is the most Subtle, Earth the most Gross of the 5 elements? Wonder of wonders, Sound is the grossest and Smell is the subtlest of them all.

The attribute of the subtlest element SPACE is SOUND the grossest attribute.

The attribute of the grossest element EARTH is SMELL the subtlest attribute.

Hear Ear Active

In the specific case of a phone call, the sense of hearing is active, others are disconnected. Hearing being linked to sound, the grossest sense, can:

- very quickly arouse intense emotion
- hurt in a manner that cannot be reversed
- cause one to form a wholly wrong notion
- make one lose control

On the other hand, in the specific case of listening to a guided meditation or a pleasant tune, the same sense can:

- heal and soothe
- make one proactive and responsible
- give a much needed direction to life
- become the game changer for success

In such situations, I am only a LISTENING BEING.

H E A R I N G is Divine. Make the effort to honor this sense.

Sight Eye Beauty

Since the universe is made up of Name (Sound) and Form (Light), the sense of seeing is again the grosser of the rest, just a notch below the sense of hearing.

Data that is assimilated just by eye, is highly prone to error or parallax. Not being aware of the fact that this is a very gross sense, making decisions only on seeing something (live, movie, image recorded or current); man makes huge mistakes, nay blunders.

At the same time, sight is powerful enough to cause complete healing, love-at-first-sight, total surrender, or any other beautiful emotion and event.

Just be aware that at this time, I am only a SEEING BEING.

S I G H T is Visionary. Go within to honor seeing.

Touch Skin Careful

Touch is placed midway in the gross to subtle band, and hence has the maximum potential.

A hug is very very potent. Kiss makes it intimate. Union.

Lots of other situations and events rely on touch for genuine appeal and authenticity. Since in a phone call, the touch attribute is entirely missing, it is not a reliable note.

During these moments, I am only a TOUCH BEING.

T O U C H is Divine. Take the time to honor touch.

Taste Tongue Delicious

Taste is a subtle sense and is hence a rarity in day to day life.

Even though food and juice and liquids are a big industry, yet taste being subtle, these are passed off by mankind as being inconsequential.

However, taste has the potential to satisfy the Soul as none else, all beings eat and fill their tummy, and this is a fundamental aspect of planet earth.

Know then, I am also a TASTE BEING.

T A S T E is marvelous. Enjoy life with great taste.

Scent Breath Subtle

Smell is placed at the far end of the spectrum and is the most subtle of all.

Proper breathing is an unknown entity. Taken for granted, it escapes everyone's serious attention.

Someday grace falls on a Being, and he does the HAPPINESS Course and the ADVANCE Course of Sri Sri Ravi Shankar.

That marks the beginning.
That surely makes for a successful ending.

First and foremost, I am a BREATH BEING.

A R O M A is subtle. Takes a while to realize this sense.

Memory Deep Emotive

Memory is layers of lives lived and perhaps of life tomorrow. Memory is impressions.

Some think it is only of the past. However the wise know it is also of the future.

The memory faculty in us can sense the future as well retrieve the past accurately. It aids in our decision making and plays a significant role in our success.

Mostly, I am lost in a MEMORY BEING.

M E M O R Y is emotion. Can be too much for the senses.

Instinct Core Body

Instinct is the body core.

Instinct rules like none else.

Instinct can be tempered and directed with excellent education.

Loving upbringing, good space, proper ambience, all serve to mold the instinct towards the finer and the nobler.

In humans it may be specific event based, but still I am an INSTINCTIVE BEING.

I N S T I N C T is pervasive. Education can Temper it right.

We are Composites

We as humans are seamless composites of these 7 Beings, each being predominant or regressive at any given moment. We live life with one or more Being dominant or submissive during day to day activity and situation.

1. At the layer level, we are composed of 7 layers in creation: **B**ody **B**reath **M**ind **I**ntellect **M**emory **E**go **S**elf.

2. At the aural level, we are combinations of the 7 chakras: **M**ooladhara **S**vadisthana **M**anipura **A**nahata **V**ishuddhi **A**jna **S**ahasrara.

3. At the cosmic level, the 7 planets exert their pulls: SURYa CHANDRa GURU SHANI MANGAL SHUKRa BUDDH.

4. At the genetic level, our DNA RNA Nuclei have the 7 stamp: ASIAN Brown AFRICAN Ebony CHINESE Yellow AMERICAN Red EUROPEAN White DRAVIDIAN Dark VIKING Blue.

5. At the geographic level, our instincts match 7 weathers: Tropical, Hot, Dry, Windy, Cold, Humid, Pleasant.

6. At the sensual level, we function due to 7 inputs to brain: SIGHT SOUND SMELL TASTE TOUCH MEMORY INSTINCT.

7. And our life-to-death milestones have the 7 stops: Baby[0+] Childhood[3+] Teen[13+] Youth[20+] Adult[30+] Mature[40+] Senior[70+].

HEARING
SEEING
TOUCHING
TASTING
SCENTING
SENSES in MEMORY LAP
ALL within INSTINCT ZONE

We are Learners

We are learning continuously, adapting, modifying, evolving. Our **Being** switches from being on study side of the table to teacher side. From being the stranger to being the boss to being the friend to being the soulmate.

We command+follow, follow+command consistently.

We are Divine

Whatever it may be,
However we may be,

Irrespective of the circumstance, situation, position:
We live on a lovely planet.
We are beautiful.
We are an orchestra, in harmony.
Life is cohesive. Romantic, Exciting, Joyful.

There is eternal grace flowing.

Epilogue

fires burning bright
flames shining bright
sunrays streaming starlight all night

the orangeYellows are a sight
the danceSwirls are so right

सर्वे भवन्तु सुखिनः । सर्वे सन्तु निरामयाः ।

सर्वे भद्राणि पश्यन्तु । मा कश्चिद् दुःख भाग्भवेत् ॥

ॐ शान्तिः शान्तिः शान्तिः ॥

When faith has blossomed in life,
Every step is led by the Divine.

Sri Sri Ravi Shankar

Om Namah Shivaya

जय गुरुदेव

www.ingramcontent.com/pod-product-compliance
Lightning Source LLC
Chambersburg PA
CBHW060923130726

48001CB00006B/2378